William Hough

The Abstract Eye:
A Photographer's Journey

Introduction

I thoroughly enjoy taking and developing abstract photographs. In the dance of light and shadow, where reality blurs into imagination, abstract photography emerges as a silent symphony. Each frame captures the ethereal, the enigmatic—the essence of moments that defy conventional boundaries. There is an anonymous quote that says "Abstract photography is a reflection of the photographer's spirit and soul." My soul and spirit are in these photographs.

Welcome to **"The Abstract Eye: A Photograpjher's Journey,"** where brushstrokes of color, geometry, and emotion collide. Whether you're an *art collector, interior designer, photography enthusiast, or corporate client*, these images will add a touch of modern elegance to any space.

In this collection, you'll encounter photographs that transcend mere representation. These abstracts beckon us to explore beyond the obvious, inviting us to lose ourselves in their ambiguity. The play of textures, the harmony of lines, and the whispers of unseen narratives—they all find refuge within these frames. Whether it's the fractured reflections on a hanging basket or the rhythmic patterns of rusted metal, each image invites contemplation. These are not just photographs; they are portals to wonder.

Abstract photography celebrates the raw elements—the interplay of light and shadow, the tension between chaos and order. Here, color becomes emotion, and form dances with abstraction. You'll witness the delicate balance of negative space, the bold strokes of minimalism, and the intricate details that pulse beneath the surface. These photographs are not bound by reality; they are whispers from the universe, urging us to see beyond the mundane.

As you turn these pages, may you find inspiration. Consider adorning your walls with these visual reveries at www. bonitaphotos.com—they are more than decor; they are conversations waiting to unfold.

Welcome to the abstract realm, where imagination dances with light.

The Photographer

William Hough, the photographer behind Bonita Photos, has been capturing and creating abstract art for over 40 years. Born in Brazil to American parents, William's work is shaped by his experiences living in seven countries across Latin America, Asia, and North America. Fluent in English, Spanish, and Portuguese, his global perspective and cultural exposure are reflected in his striking abstract compositions, which span subjects like nature, urban decay, graffiti, textiles, and everyday objects.

In 2005, William founded Bonita Photos (www.bonitaphotos.com) to showcase his diverse portfolio. His career highlights include being invited to Venice in 2009 for commercial photography and having his piece "The Wailing Wall" added to the prestigious private collection of Joseph and Toby Tanenbaum in 2012. William's works have been exhibited in Wynwood, Miami (2015), and at the Kendall Art Center in Miami (2016), where his photograph *The Rainbow Woman* is now part of the permanent collection.

William's carefully curated abstract collection is known for its ability to evoke a wide range of emotions—peace, curiosity, joy, and introspection—through bold colors and intricate patterns. His work emphasizes the beauty of personal interpretation, allowing viewers to create their own meanings and emotional connections. Abstract art, as William presents it, is more than just visual appeal; it's an invitation to engage, interpret, and reflect. Whether displayed as a statement piece in a home, office, or gallery, his art offers both aesthetic beauty and endless opportunities for conversation.

In addition to his exhibitions, William has produced six photography books and is currently revising an eBook titled *Gotcha, Click! A Humanist's Guide to Street Photography*. Explore more of William's captivating abstracts at Bonita Photos (www.bonitaphotos.com).

Calm & Contemplation

Brilliant Simplicity

Dubrovnik, Croatia

Often the simple impacts us with its beauty and calm. These colors on a wall was a blend of sea, earth and mountains. "Brilliant Simplicity," captured from a wall in Dubrovnik, Croatia, is a striking abstract composition that juxtaposes warm and cool tones to create a visually captivating piece. The central area, dominated by bright orange fading into yellow, contrasts beautifully with the cool-toned section on the right, featuring speckles of blue and hints of purple. The thick, tactile texture suggests an impasto technique, adding depth and dimension.

Felicia

Moscow, Russia

Felicia's beauty brings longing into my soul and being, and my remaining youth languishes with desire.

"Felicia" weaves emotion through color and form. The backdrop—a gradient of deep reds and purples—mirrors the mix of passion and melancholy. Imagine standing before it—the curves, like whispered secrets, draw you in. They flow, smooth yet restless, hinting at unfulfilled desires.

But there's more: a solitary figure, shades of blue and orange, suspended above the curves. Is it a memory, a dream, or a longing heart? The contrast against the dark background intensifies its isolation. Each viewer interprets—their own ache, their own story.

Growth of Light
Monaco

—

Growth of Light" captures the essence of illumination's organic expansion, transforming a simple light filament into a profound metaphor for the spread of knowledge and ideas.

The image, taken in Monaco, showcases the filament's intricate, dendritic pattern against a stark black background, evoking natural growth processes like tree branches or leaf veins.

This juxtaposition of artificial and natural elements invites viewers to contemplate the interplay between human innovation and nature's inherent patterns.

7

La Dehesa

Santiago, Chile

It was a dark and sad day in La Dehesa, east of Santiago, Chile. I was waiting for a client in an old library, next to a wine cupboard. This dusty stone was sitting on the bookshelf. I polished it, cleaned it and was amazed by its beauty. Brightened my day!!

Dominated by golden yellow hues, the photograph suggests the sun's embrace during the magical golden hour. It's as if sunlight dances across the canvas, infusing energy into every pixel.

La Dehesa captures the essence of light, texture, and movement—a visual symphony.

8

Marble Elegance

Rio de Janeiro, Brazil

Marbled Elegance is a captivating exploration of natural beauty and intricate detail. This close–up image captures the essence of a natural stone marble, with a rich tapestry of colors and textures that evoke a sense of depth and complexity. The dominant color palette is a serene blue, reminiscent of the sky or sea, interlaced with veins of gold and white that suggest an organic fluidity.

These golden lines are bold and meandering, creating natural pathways that draw the eye across the image. The abstract qualities of this photograph are pronounced in the way these elements combine to form emotional resonance.

9

Placid
Miami, Florida

Rubell Museum has been the home of many famous artists. This photograph was taken of the floor where many walked, talked, painted and created. The abstract produces beauty and calm.

"Placid" evokes a serene tranquility, a gentle repose in hues and textures. Dominated by cool blues, it suggests a calm, soothing atmosphere. A burst of warm yellow and pink at the top interrupts this coolness, like the first light of dawn breaking through a misty morning sky. The colors bleed into one another, creating soft edges that enhance the dreamlike quality of the piece.

Rose Petals on Yellow

Sydney, Australia

—

Rose petals fill the senses with color and perfume, producing calm and peace.

Abstract photography often emphasizes shapes, forms, colors, and textures over the literal representation of reality.

In this image, the focus is on the vibrant red rose petals scattered across a textured yellow background. The strong contrast between the red and yellow, along with the play on textures and patterns, create a visually striking effect.

The image does not immediately reveal the context or scale of the objects, inviting viewers to interpret it in their own way.

Strings

Miami, Florida

—

Our paths are parallel to each other, but too often we don't cross paths or connect, and we live in solitude. We need closeness and relationships. This striking composition features a stark white background, elegantly intersected by fluid, organic lines in bold red.

These crimson lines exhibit delightful variations in thickness and curvature, creating a sense of dynamic movement and depth. Some lines are densely packed, hinting at intensity, while others flow more freely, providing breathing space.

Amidst this vibrant red dance, a singular green stripe stands out—a beacon of simplicity and contrast. Its presence draws the eye, serving as a focal point within the composition. foreground and background.

12

The Fly
Monaoo

Went into a small bookstore in Monaco that sold a sundry of items. Lost in the cluster was this Fly. It's become one of my favorite photographs.

Ordinary materials transform into an extraordinary object. Craftsmanship shines through—each detail meticulously considered.The use of focus is masterful. Sharp where it matters, while the extended fibers blur softly into the background. It suggests motion, freezing a moment in time. Primarily orange and white against black—a dramatic palette. All eyes on the subject. The reflective surface beneath adds depth, hinting at an ethereal realm.

Sands of Time

Miami, Florida

Solid time has rapidly filled out the past, but we can see both the excitement and movement in our futures. This photograph was taken from a piece of painted graffiti in Wynwood of Miami.

The vibrant orange-red hue symbolizes the passage of time. It's as if the sands themselves have absorbed the sun's warmth and history. The granular surface invites touch, hinting at the countless experiences etched into its fabric. Each grain tells a story—a footprint, a whispered secret, a forgotten dream.

Interspersed white streaks disrupt the monochrome canvas. These moments of clarity stand out against the continuous flow of time, like memories that refuse to fade.

The Sheikh's Robe

Marrakech, Morocco

—

While walking through a plaza in Marrakesh, I saw a small table with delicate fabrics. I felt them and touched their softness and mystery. The soft nobility and exquisite color of this royal fabric is definitely suitable for a sheikh's robe.

The Sheikh's Robe" features a richly textured fabric, draped and folded in a way that creates dynamic lines and shadows.

The tapestry of hues ranges from deep blues and vibrant yellows to subtle hints of green and speckles of red, each color blending seamlessly into the next. This interplay of colors and textures evokes a sense of movement and depth, making the fabric appear almost alive.

White Rivers
Qingdao, China

While visiting Qingdao, China along the beach, I saw markings on a wall. It's is a stunning example of abstract photography that captivates with its interplay of form and color.

The image features jagged, angular shapes that resemble shards of glass or ice, with crisp edges and pointed tips. These predominantly white shapes are set against a rich, cobalt blue background, creating a striking contrast that immediately draws the viewer's eye. The beauty of "White River" lies in its ability to evoke a sense of movement and fluidity despite its geometric rigidity.

Energy, Movement & Vitality

Aurora Ignis
Concepcion, Chile

Aurora Ignis is derived from Latin, meaning "Dawn of Fire." This photograph evokes a fiery dawn, capturing a vibrant and dynamic essence. I was at the University of Concepcion and saw this light from a bulb shining through a piece of cloth.

The abstract nature of this photograph allows for a deeply personal experience, to project thoughts and emotions onto the image. This visual texture and evocative interplay between warmth and coolness, makes this photograph a standout addition to any collection of abstract art. It not only captures the eye, but also engages the mind, encouraging a meditative exploration of its depths

18

Before the Revolution

Istanbul, Turkey

This splattered paint was on the ground in an alley way in Istanbul. I had just passed a bridge with a burning car. The red, which pulses with tension, reminded me of the possible coming bloodshed and maybe revolution, but the blue showed that there was still hope.

Vivid reds dominate, like flames licking at change. Cyan splashes offer respite—a cool breath before upheaval. The black markings hint at secrets, whispers of rebellion.
A white line, slightly off–center, cleaves the canvas. Is it a barrier or a bridge? The moment before transformation—the calm before chaos.

19

Captivating Orchid

Manila, Philippines

—

Captivating Orchid is a mesmerizing abstract where fiery reds and oranges dance harmoniously, creating a warm and dynamic visual experience. The central focus rests on circular shapes reminiscent of droplets or bubbles, set against a textured background that hints at organic or cellular structures. These luminous droplets exhibit lighter edges, suggesting three–dimensional forms caught in motion.

What makes Captivating Orchid special is its intense color palette, evoking passion and energy. The rhythmic repetition of shapes adds balance, while strategic blurs create an illusion of depth.

20

Door to Discovery
Madrid, Spain

—

This colorful top of an old door in Spain tempted all passerbys to open it and peek inside. The discovery could be staid and old or dynamic and full of new possibilities.

The canvas bursts forth with shades of green and red, interwoven like a secret garden waiting to be unveiled. The rough, weathered texture hints at the passage of time, as if this door has witnessed countless stories. But what truly sets this abstract apart is the vertical line—subtle yet powerful—slightly left of center. It's the threshold, the hinge between the known and the unknown. As our eyes trace its contours, we wonder: What lies beyond?

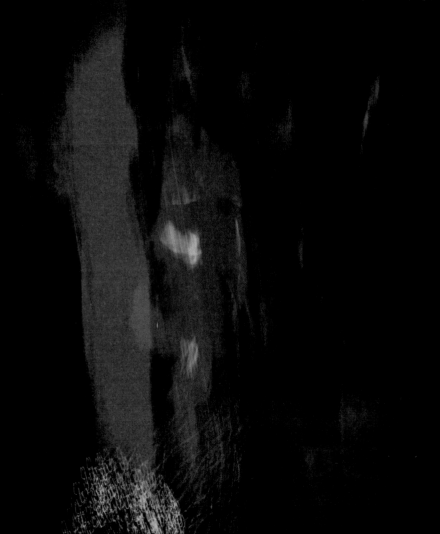

Ecstacy
London, United Kingdom

Went into a girlie bar in London, filled with low lights and smothering smoke. The music was loud, fast and raw. I surreptitiously took this photograph under the nose of a rather massive bouncer. "Ecstasy" emerges as a visual symphony—an ode to abstract expression. The photograph vibrates with passion, a bold splash of crimson that ignites the senses. But this artwork is more than mere color; it's a conversation between hues, a dance of reds and purples that swirl and blur, defying boundaries.

"Ecstasy" defies definition. It's the heartbeat of a moment frozen in motion; a fleeting encounter captured forever. The lines blur, inviting interpretation. Is it the pulse of music, the laughter of patrons, or the touch of a stranger's hand? Perhaps it's all of these—an invitation to lose ourselves in the chaos, to find meaning in the abstract.

Flourishing Fertility

Boston, Massachusetts
—

A flower was fully blooming with glorious colors and shapes, a celebration of life and growth. This is full of hope and life and vitality.

Dominated by warm yellows—sunlight's embrace—and cool blues, the photograph dances with energy. It's as if seasons collide, birthing new possibilities.

Each mark pulses with vitality, urging us to witness creation. At the center, a yellow shape blooms—an entity of fertility. Is it a flower, a cosmic birth, or a soul awakening? Interpretations abound.

Exploding Flower

Newburyport. Massachusetts

—

This blossoming flower, which was exploding with new shoots and color, depicts fertility, hope and the vibrancy of life.

The composition is a harmonious blend of blues, greens, pinks, and reds, creating a cool yet intense atmosphere that draws the eye and invites contemplation. The myriad linear elements radiating outward from a central point suggest rapid movement and growth, evoking a sense of organic dynamism.

24

Electro Dance

Monaco

Life is synonymous with pulsating rhythms. I opened a door to a nightclub, and this is what I saw.

Electro Dance captures the mesmerizing interplay of light and energy within a plasma globe. Vibrant blue and purple electrical streams emanate from the central sphere, creating an intricate dance of light that resembles lightning frozen in time. The central sphere glows warmly, serving as the nucleus for this electric ballet.

This abstract piece showcases the beauty of physics in action. It is a perfect blend of science and art.

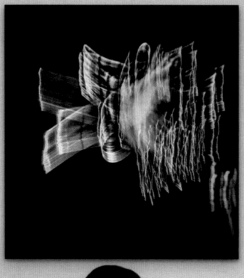

Electro Rhythms

Monaco

Electro Rhythms captured in Monaco, is a vibrant abstract piece that embodies the essence of motion and energy. The image features a dynamic, flowing structure with vibrant blue and yellow hues against a dark background.
å
At its center, a spherical shape with concentric patterns extends into multiple lines and waves radiating outward, creating an impression of movement and rhythm.

This visual representation of light patterns evokes the sensation of music or sound waves, transforming auditory experiences into a striking visual form.

Havana Dangles
Havana, Cuba

───

Havana Dangles" is a photograph of dangles in a Havana market. It presents a close-up view of elongated, vertical glass elements with a translucent quality. These dangling forms are adorned with intricate embossed patterns and textures each catching and refracting light in its unique way.

What makes "Havana Dangles" special is its dynamic array of colors that seem to dance across the image, evoking the tropical vibrancy reminiscent of Havana's lively culture. The abstract nature lies in its focus on form, texture, and color over any identifiable subject matter. Salient features include the varying degrees of transparency in the dangling objects, their diverse embossed designs adding depth.

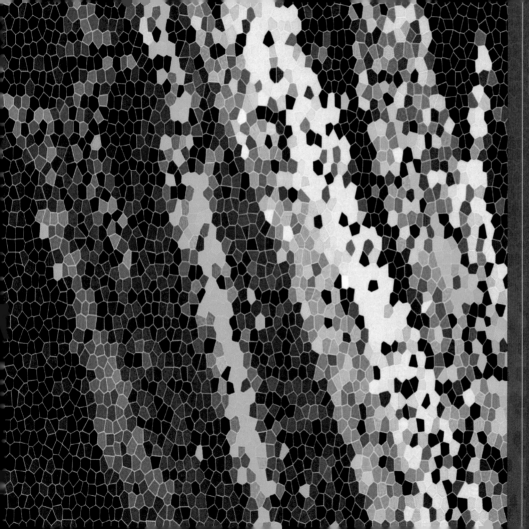

Kaleidoscopic Diamonds

Chichén Itzá. Mexico

"Kaleidoscopic Diamonds" is a creation from bright color textiles and blankets being sold in Chichen Itza in Mexico. The colors generated were manipulated to create the kaleidoscope.

The composition consists of numerous small, hexagonal shapes that fit together like pieces of a puzzle, creating a tapestry of color that is both chaotic and harmonious. The hexagons vary in size, which adds depth and complexity to the image, suggesting a three–dimensional quality as if one could reach out and feel the texture created by the varying shapes.

Each turn of this metaphorical kaleidoscope reveals new alignments and combinations, making the image an endless source of fascination.

Le Tableau
Cannes, France
—

"Le Tableau" was the top of a colorful old table I saw in Cannes, France. The vibrant textures and colors that transcend its mundane origins becomes a piece of abstract art. The photograph captures the essence of peeling paint. The dominant colors are shades of yellow and red, with hints of the natural wood color peeking through where the paint has chipped away. This interplay creates a dynamic tension within the frame, as if the layers of paint are in conversation with each other.

What makes "The Table" particularly striking is its ability to evoke different emotions and interpretations. The rough texture created by the peeling layers adds depth and complexity, causes speculation of the passage of time and the stories embedded within this seemingly simple table.

29

Psychedelic Goddess

Coral Gables, Florida

—

This psychedelic goddess has a look of vision and future thoughts. She is a muse for all. In "Psychedelic Goddess", the interplay of vibrant blues and yellows creates an arresting visual rhythm.

The composition resembles microscopic cellular structures, inviting viewers to explore a hidden universe. The seamless blending of colors adds depth, while strategically placed blurs evoke movement and energy. This abstract balances chaos and harmony, making it a thought–provoking piece.

Solar Plasma

Shenzhen, China

This smudge of paint on a wall reminded me of the sun's important role in the universe and throughout the history of man.

In Solar Plasma, fiery oranges and reds collide, creating an intense visual symphony. The thick, impasto strokes evoke raw emotion, as if the canvas itself pulses with energy. The play of light on the ridges and valleys adds depth, making the painting almost three-dimensional. This abstract masterpiece transcends representation—it's not about objects or scenes; it's about the fervor of color and form. One can feel the heat, the urgency, and the unbridled creativity that birthed this extraordinary work.

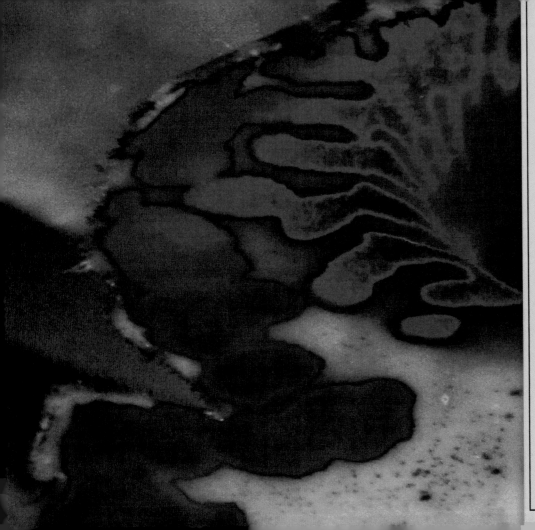

Surreal Piano

Zengzheng, China

—

"Surreal Piano" merges visual art with the conceptual feeling of music. Imagine standing before it—the vibrant red patterns, like flames or flowing lava, dance against a green and yellow backdrop.

The edges, highlighted in bright yellow, pulse with energy. The blues and oranges add depth—the keys of an otherworldly piano. Each stroke, each curve, resonates. It's as if the music itself spills into the photograph.

"Surreal Piano" invites introspection, serenity, and a symphony of imagination.

Thailand Entanglements

Bangkok, Thailand

—

I took a close up of this basket hanging in a market in Bangkok. It is a complex and intricate web of basket weaves which looks like metallic lines . The tangles resemble a chaotic dance of wires, each contributing to an overall tapestry.

Dominant shades of blue and orange create a vibrant contrast, evoking energy and curiosity. The lines vary in thickness, from delicate strands to thicker bands, adding texture and interest. Light seems to refract through translucent patches, suggesting hidden depths within the chaos.

Thailand Entanglements captures a frozen moment of beauty—an industrial coldness juxtaposed with organic warmth.

33

The Awakening of Prometheus

New York, New York

The splendid and vibrant colors of this graffiti in an alley in New York City (near Waverly Place) made me feel what Prometheus had felt when he envisioned giving humanity one of our greatest gifts: fire. It's full of hope. Dominated by intense red hues, interspersed with splashes of yellow, green, and blue, the rough, layered texture suggests an energetic and passionate application of paint, evoking a sense of awakening or rebirth.

This dynamic composition, invites open interpretation and stirs emotions, reflecting the mythological figure Prometheus's association with creativity and rebellion, symbolizing the powerful resurgence of ideas and innovation.

The Brass

New York, City, New York

—

Nothing like a NY parade. The brass of the tuba was shiny and bright as it harrumphed down 5th Avenue, reflecting light and life.

The Brass features a blend of warm golden tones with hints of other colors and showcases a variety of shapes and textures that don't immediately represent any specific object or scene. The swirls and irregular patterns create a sense of movement, making the image dynamic and visually engaging.

Tin Can

Marrakesh, Morocco

Next to one of the many plazas in Marrakesh, a brightly painted can was thrown in a corner. The colors and form dazzled me. I took a close–up to capture the excitement and beauty.

It features a vibrant array of colors, including vivid reds, blues, purples, and whites, with patterns that resemble streaks and bubbles. The rich color saturation and the fluid, almost organic patterns, give the photograph a dynamic and lively appearance. Abstract photography often focuses on shapes, colors, and textures, and this image does just that, inviting viewers to interpret it in their own way.

The Swirl
Istanbul, Turkey

While in a mall in Istanbul, I walked by a column with a metal band, reflecting the lights and color of the shops and stores..

The image is a mesmerizing composition of fluid, undulating shapes and a rich tapestry of colors that bleed into one another, creating an almost hypnotic effect. The swirls seem to dance across the photograph. This dynamic quality is one of the image's most compelling attributes; it imbues the static photograph with a sense of life and energy.

Three Curls
Knossos, Crete

This abstract artwork, originating from a Minoan palace in Crete and dating back 4,000 years, vividly captures the essence of Minoan artistry. The warm hues of red, orange, and yellow, combined with intricate plant–like motifs and sinuous, wave–like patterns, reflect the Minoans' deep connection to nature and the sea.

The dynamic fluidity and organic growth depicted in the piece evoke the labyrinthine structures and ceremonial spaces that characterized Minoan architecture. This artwork stands as a testament to the sophisticated aesthetic sensibilities and spiritual depth of one of the earliest advanced civilizations.

This is Life
Massachusetts, USA

This tree was teeming with a very unusual color combination of Life found in Nature in front of my house.
What a wonderful planet!

Dominated by shades of purple, the photograph exudes both vibrancy and mystery. Imagine standing close, feeling the granular texture under your fingertips—a tactile journey through abstract realms.

The composition dances with contrasts: vivid purples juxtaposed against bright yellow spots. These irregular shapes create a dynamic rhythm, like life's unpredictable moments. The lines blur, hinting at movement and change.

Time Light Dimension

Medellin, Colombia

This blend of lights and time creates a dimension, also called the First Dimension.

Time Light Dimension is a mesmerizing composition that seamlessly blends light, color, and form. The image features dynamic, curved light strips set against a darker background. These illuminated strips evoke a sense of movement, as if they are bending through space and time. The vibrant blue and yellow hues create a striking contrast, while the metallic structures provide texture and complexity. What sets this abstract apart is its ability to convey depth and dimensionality within a two-dimensional frame,

40

Reflection & Serenity

Focus
Miami, Florida

Everything has a center or nexus around which all evolves or flows. This photo was taken from the floor of the famous Rubell Gallery in Miami where many artists have painted or developed various works of art. This is one of the marks that remain.

The central yellow circle stands out sharply against a backdrop of blue and red hues with white streaks, symbolizing the journey from chaos to clarity. The rough, grainy textures surrounding the focal point represent the layers of distraction and confusion that we often navigate through. As the eye is drawn to the vivid center, it mirrors the process of focusing in on what truly matters amidst the noise.

Cave Wall

Medellin, Colombia

Cave Wall captures the essence of an abstract photograph through its rich texture and warm, earthy color palette. The photograph showcases a close–up view of a cave wall, emphasizing the natural patterns and hues that make it unique. The surface is a tapestry of sienna, burnt umber, and ochre tones mingled with patches of lighter creams and whites. A prominent feature is the deep crack running vertically down the center, adding to the rugged character of the image. Speckles and scratches are scattered across the canvas, suggesting age and exposure to elements over time.

What makes this abstract special is its ability to evoke a sense of ancient history and geological processes without depicting them directly. The interplay between light and shadow enhances the three–dimensional feel of the uneven surface.

Longing
Paris, France

"Longing" dances on the edge of reality, a symphony of color and shadow. The photograph is a twilight dreamscape—a fusion of deep crimson and midnight indigo. Imagine the brushstrokes of a cosmic painter, swirling nebulae into existence. The electric blue streak, like a comet's tail, slices through the composition, defying gravity and logic.

The interplay of curves and angles is deliberate—an ode to chaos and order. The smooth arcs invite introspection, while jagged edges jolt the senses awake. This abstract whispers secrets: the warmth of forgotten sunsets, the chill of distant galaxies.

"Longing" isn't merely decor; it's an emotional catalyst. Hang it in your living room, and conversations will veer from weather to cosmic mysteries. Place it in an office, and deadlines will blur as minds wander.

Iona

Punto del Este, Uruguay

—

This beautiful face was part of a street photography captured in Punto del Este, then combined with an abstract. She is beautiful, friendly and purposeful.

Iona is a blend of abstract and representational art. The facial features are recognizable, but they are intertwined with expressive, colorful, and loosely defined elements that create a dreamlike, abstract composition. The abstract patterns and vibrant colors surrounding the face contribute to a sense of artistic interpretation, leaving room for personal reflection and interpretation, which are key aspects of abstract art.

Mind Terrain

Miami, Florida

Mind Terrain is a vibrant amalgamation of colors and textures taken from a wall in Miami—an abstract cartography of thoughts and emotions. Imagine tracing your fingers across its surface: warm golds and yellows intermingle with cool blues and bold pinks. The textures shift— smooth washes meet gritty patches like memories etched into neural pathways.

But it's the linear details that intrigue—the thin red fissures or boundaries. Are they fault lines or bridges? The canvas whispers stories of wear, resilience, and the duality of cognition. Each hue represents a facet of the mind's complex terrain, and the interplay invites contemplation.

Orange Lady

Punta del Este, Uruguay.

—

In a furtive moment, a lovely woman relaxes with a drink and quiet thoughts. All living creatures need this moment.

While there are discernible elements like the suggestion of a face, the image's overall composition, with its intense colors, stylized contours, and surreal blending, leans more towards abstraction. The title hints at a subject, but the execution focuses more on mood and artistic expression than on detailed representation, making it an abstract work.

Rainbow Woman
Valparaiso, Chile

The image, a composite photograph, features a blend of vibrant colors, geometric patterns, and textures layered over a human form. While the figure is somewhat recognizable, the abstract treatment—through the use of bold colors, stylized lines, and a fragmented visual approach—transforms it into a conceptual work that emphasizes mood, emotion, and interpretation over realism.

This kind of abstraction plays with both representational and non-representational elements, allowing viewers to engage with the art on multiple levels, whether through its aesthetic qualities, symbolic interpretations, or the emotions it evokes.

Rainbow Woman is now a permanent part of the Kendall Art Gallery Collection in Miami.

River of Gold
Miami, Florida

—

The search for gold and riches resides in the hearts of all men and women. This photograph was taken of the floor of Rubell Museum where many famous artists walked, talked, painted and created.

It features a blend of colors with no discernible objects or figures. The central area is blurred, surrounded by more vivid and defined patches of blue, yellow, and red hues that seem to be digitally altered or painted in an expressive manner. The vibrant color palette and the contrast between the focused and unfocused areas create a visually engaging and interpretive image.

River of Gold,
Miami, Florida (Left)

The search for gold and riches resides in the hearts of all men and women. This photograph was taken of the floor of Rubell Museun where many famous artists walked, talked, painted and created.

Thailand Entanglements
*Bangkok Thailand (*Middle*)*

In a Thai market, this basket, hanging from the ceiling, looked futuristic with neural connections.

Captivating Orchid
Manila, Phillipines (Right)

The brilliant colors and life of the orchid capture all.

Notes

The abstract photographs can be purchased at bonitaphotos.com. If you don't see the abstract on the website, please inquire at bill@bonitaphotos.com.

Satisfaction Guaranteed

All photos are 100% satisfaction guaranteed.
Our ultimate goal is your complete satisfaction. If, for any reason, you are not thrilled with the final photograph, we will work tirelessly to make it right. We are committed to your happiness and will go above and beyond to ensure you are 100% satisfied with the results. Also, we will do our best to provide very large sizes you may require.

Contact: William Hough

Email: bill@bonitaphotos.com

Web: www. bonitaphotos.com

William Hough

The End

The Abstract Eye: A Photographer's Journey

This collection of stunning abstract photographs is designed to captivate and inspire. Whether you're **an art collector, interior designer, photography enthusiast, or corporate client**, these images will add a touch of modern elegance to any space.

Each photograph transforms everyday moments into extraordinary works of art. Through a unique blend of color, texture, and emotion, these pieces invite you to see the world from new, captivating perspectives. The interplay of light, shadow, and form speaks to both timeless and contemporary themes, resonating with viewers of all tastes.

Inspired by the hidden beauty in textures and forms, hopefully, these works will encourage the viewer to pause, reflect, and discover meaning in the abstract. These images invite exploration beyond the surface, creating a visual and emotional experience that transcends the ordinary.

Join me in celebrating the art of abstraction, and let these photographs bring new perspectives. Explore more and purchase these abstract works at www.bonitaphotos.com.

William Hough

Email: bill@bonitaphotos.com

Web: www.bonitaphotos.com

Made in the USA
Las Vegas, NV
16 November 2024